Hamad Bin Khalifa University Press
P O Box 5825
Doha, Qatar

www.hbkupress.com

All rights reserved.

No part of this publication may be reproduced or transmitted in any form or by any means, electronic or mechanical, including photocopying, recording, or any information storage or retrieval system, without prior permission in writing from the publishers.

No responsibility for loss caused to any individual or organization acting on or refraining from action as a result of the material in this publication can be accepted by HBKU Press or the author.

First English edition in 2023

ISBN: 9789927161582

Printed in Doha-Qatar.

Qatar National Library Cataloging-in-Publication (CIP)

Eissa, Amal, author.

Mutaz Barshim : winning beyond gold! / by Amal Eissa ; illustrations by Maria Al-Mahoozi. First English edition. – Doha, Qatar : Hamad Bin Khalifa University Press, 2023.

24 pages : color illustrations ; 24 cm

ISBN 978-992-716-158-2

1. Barsham, Mutaz, 1991- -- Juvenile literature. 2. Hurdling (Track and field) -- Qatar -- Biography -- Juvenile literature. 3. Children's stories, English. 4. Picture books. 5. Biographies. I. Al-Mahoozi, Maria, illustrator. II. Title.

GV1067. E47 2023
796.4 – dc 23   202328639406

Mutaz Barshim

Winning Beyond Gold!

By Amal Eissa

Illustrations by Maria AL-Mahoozi

Hello!

Hello! My name is Mutaz Barshim, and I'm an Olympic High Jumper from Qatar. During my career I won many gold medals.

Training takes a lot of time and effort!
Olympic sports aren't easy.

With God's grace and my hard work, I became one of the best in the world! It's an honor to bring gold medals home to my wonderful country, Qatar.

Winning makes me feel happy and joyful.
It's the reward for all my hard work.

Does anything feel better than winning?

In the Tokyo 2020 Olympics, I competed against many good athletes from all over the world. In the final round, I had to compete against my Italian friend **Gianmarco Tamberi** for the gold medal.

TOKYO 2020

The competition was tough, and we kept getting tied!

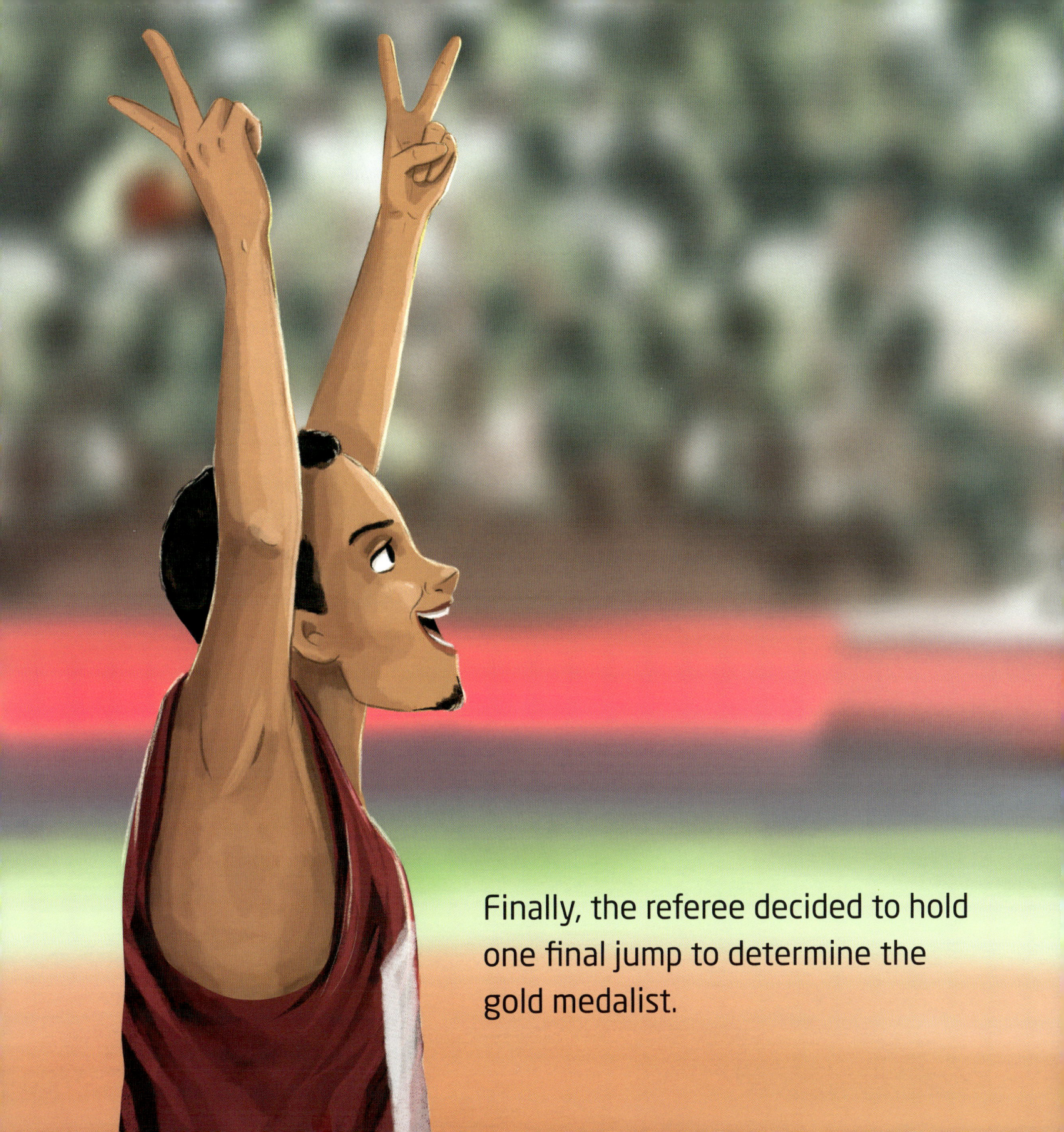

Finally, the referee decided to hold one final jump to determine the gold medalist.

I then remembered the question I used to ask myself all the time: "Does anything feel better than winning?"
Yes! The joy of sharing and celebrating with others does.

So I said to myself, "Why shouldn't we win together?"

We decided to share the victory.
I turned to the referee and asked,
"Could we share the gold medal?"
"Yes, if you want to!" He replied.

He then gave us two gold medals.
My friend jumped up to hug me with a big smile.

I've never felt happier! This felt so much better than just winning by myself. It is the joy of **sharing with others** that brings true happiness.

Also available in Arabic